basketball's new wave

Vince Carter

The Fire Burns Bright

BY

MARK STEWART

THE MILLBROOK PRESS
BROOKFIELD, CONNECTICUT

M

THE MILLBROOK PRESS

Produced by
BITTERSWEET PUBLISHING
John Sammis, President
and
TEAM STEWART, INC.
RESEARCHED AND EDITED BY MIKE KENNEDY

Series Design and Electronic Page Makeup by
JAFFE ENTERPRISES
Ron Jaffe

All photos courtesy AP/ Wide World Photos, Inc. except the following:
SportsChrome USA: Brian Spurlock, photographer — Cover
Marquette University — Page 9
Daytona Beach News-Journal — Pages 10, 13
University of North Carolina — Pages 15, 16, 24
Robert Crawford — Page 17
The following images are from the collection of Team Stewart:
Student Sports (© 1994) — Page 14
Upper Deck — Pages 32 (© 1999), 37 (© 2000)
NBA Properties, Inc. (© 2000) — Page 39
Time, Inc. (© 2000)— Page 44

Printed in the United States of America

Published by
The Millbrook Press, Inc.
2 Old New Milford Road
Brookfield, Connecticut   06804

www.millbrookpress.com

Library of Congress Cataloging-in-Publication Data

Stewart, Mark.
    Vince Carter : the fire burns bright / by Mark Stewart.
        p. cm. — (Basketball's new wave)
    Includes index.
    ISBN 0-7613-2270-1 (lib. bdg.). 0-7613-1499-7 (pbk)
      1. Carter, Vince—Juvenile literature. 2. Basketball players—United
States—Biography—Juvenile literature. [1. Carter, Vince. 2. Basketball players. 3.
African Americans—Biography] I. Title. II. Series.
GV884.C39 S74 2001
796.323'092—dc21
[B]
                                                                    00-067871

1 3 5 7 9 10 8 6 4 2

Contents

Doctor in the House

chapter 1

"Even as an infant, he would get impatient real easy."

— **MICHELLE CARTER-ROBINSON**

When auto-racing fans think of Daytona Beach, Florida, they picture the Daytona 500, the biggest event on the NASCAR schedule. When college students think of Daytona Beach, they picture the wild times of spring break. When Vince Carter thinks about Daytona Beach, he thinks about home. According to Vince, his hometown is not always packed with racing fans or partying teenagers. Most of the time, in fact, it is kind of quiet. "Daytona is not like your typical city," he says. "It's not Miami, it's not Orlando. It's a little slower."

Of course, Vince was not your typical kid, either. He was born on January 26, 1977, and long before he could walk—and long before he dribbled his first basketball (at the age of two)—he always seemed to have somewhere he needed to go or something he had to do. It was as if something was pulling Vince all the time. Games became a big part of his life. Vince loved to compete in sports, especially basketball, and he

Vince's mother plants a kiss on his cheek as he accepts the NBA Rookie of the Year award. Michelle Carter-Robinson says her son has had that "extra burst" of energy since he was an infant.

> *"My parents are my inspiration. Believe it or not, they're my personal coaches. After every game I still call them and get their take on how I played."*
>
> **VINCE CARTER**

adored his video games. At the age of six, he could hardly imagine needing anything else in his life. "As long as I had a court, some video games, and something to eat at night, I was happy," he recalls.

During this time, there was a lot of arguing in the Carter home. It scared Vince and his brother, Chris, when their father yelled at their mother, Michelle. They did not understand what the problem was. When Vince was in second grade, his parents got a divorce. Things calmed down immediately. Michelle, Vince, and Chris made a good team.

Soon, a fourth person joined the team. His name was Harry Robinson. Like Michelle, he was a teacher, so they had a lot in common. Harry loved Vince and Chris, too. He and Michelle were married. To this day, Vince considers Harry his "real" father.

Harry and Michelle tried to get Vince to focus his boundless energy on achieving certain goals and making the most of his free time. At first, Vince wanted to spend all of his free time playing basketball.

His favorite player was Julius

Did You Know?

Vince's exposure to different kinds of music as a child shaped his tastes as an adult. Today, he listens to a little bit of everything. "Wherever I hear music," he says, "no matter what it is, I just listen."

Erving of the Philadelphia 76ers, who won the NBA championship when Vince was in first grade. Doctor J seemed to defy the laws of gravity. When he drove toward the

Julius Erving's ability to hang in the air and create made him Vince's favorite player.

basket, he was able to rise a full head above the defense. Once in the air, he could roll the ball off his fingertips, bank it off the backboard, or continue his flight right to the rim and throw the ball down through the hoop. Vince also noticed that Erving played with poise and determination, and was always under control. Vince wanted to be just like Doctor J.

Vince would practice these moves in the playground. He could not get anywhere near the rim, of course, but he was able to leap much higher than the other boys. Soon his friends gave him a nickname: "UFO"—which stood for unidentified flying object.

With his parents guiding him, Vince also did well in school. He was clever, outgoing, and was not afraid to take chances. Harry, a school band director, encouraged Vince to experiment with music. First, he played the alto saxophone, then the tenor saxophone, then the trumpet, and then the drums. Vince liked the drums. He could make a lot of noise, work off a lot of energy, and because he was in charge of keeping the beat, he felt like he was in control of all the other musicians.

Above the Rim

"He was always a ham on the court. Then after the game he would change back to being a quiet, humble guy."

— CORI BROWN, CHILDHOOD FRIEND

Around the age of 11, Vince Carter began living up to his nickname, UFO. He measured just a few inches over 5 feet (152 centimeters) tall, yet he could already jump up and reach the rim. By the age of 12, he was no longer "unidentified"—everyone in Daytona Beach had heard of him. A regular at the city courts, Vince was one of the top pickup players in town. Big crowds would gather when he played, waiting for the little guy to do one of his famous dunks.

The first thing spectators noticed about Vince was that there was much more to his game than monster jams. For a seventh grader, he seemed to understand a lot about basketball's finer points. Vince had his Uncle Oliver to thank for that. Right around the time Vince was born, Oliver Lee was starting his college basketball career at Marquette University in Wisconsin. One of the best high-school players in Florida, Lee accepted a scholarship from Marquette and became its top scorer and rebounder by his senior

Vince's uncle, Oliver Lee, goes up strong for Marquette. He took Vince under his wing when he returned to Daytona Beach.

year. He was drafted by the Chicago Bulls in 1981, but could not catch on with the pros. Lee returned to Daytona and played in the local leagues. Vince remembers watching him as a kid, and later working with his uncle on his game. "He sort of took me under his wing and taught me a lot," Vince says.

Vince's parents knew he had a future in basketball, and supported him at every turn. They made sure he never neglected his schoolwork, and encouraged him to keep up with his music. They also told him to always be himself. When Vince was young and wanted to wear Michael Jordan's number 23, they suggested he choose another number and make it famous. Vince picked number 15, the one he wears today.

When Vince was 14, he was wearing the uniform of the Mainland High School Buccaneers freshman basketball team. He took to high-school ball right away, learning how to set up complex plays and how to position himself in a zone defense. Mainland's opponents double-teamed Vince every time he ran down the court, but every so often he broke loose for a twisting layup or thunderous dunk. In one game, Vince took the ball to the hoop and left his feet a little earlier than usual. Thinking he would shoot the ball on the way down, Vince was shocked to find that he kept going higher and higher. He slammed the ball into the basket with tremendous force, rattling the backboard

Vince soars above his opponents to grab a one-handed rebound in a high-school game.

and bringing the fans to their feet. The players on both sides just stood around trying to understand what they had just seen. The refs had to remind everyone there was still a game to play!

During the summer of 1992, Vince worked several hours every day to get himself ready to move up to the Mainland varsity team. He devoted much time to developing the lefthanded part of his game. By the fall he could dribble and shoot equally well with either hand—he was practically ambidextrous! Vince won a starting job on the varsity and averaged 20 points a game. He was still growing into his body, which was now more than 6 feet (183 cm) tall, so there were times when he felt a bit awkward. But when he had his game together, he was almost impossible to stop.

Vince and several of his teammates decided to attend a basketball camp across the state in Tallahassee the following summer. They thought it was a good idea to learn new skills and strategies together, so they could improve as a team. At this camp, Vince first realized how good he could be. He seemed to experience everything at a slightly different speed than the other boys, and he felt his personality come out during the games, as if playing basketball were the most natural and comfortable thing he could do.

Vince's teammates noticed this change, too. He would take over games in the most dramatic ways. In one contest, Vince injured his right wrist. The trainer taped it up and sent him back into the game, but the wrap was too tight for him to shoot right-handed. So he simply did everything letfhanded. When the final buzzer sounded, Vince had scored 34 points, including five lefthanded three-pointers!

Mainland's 1993–1994 season was one for the record books. Coach Charlie Brinkerhoff decided to move Vince, who was now almost 6 feet 6 inches (198 cm) tall, from his natural guard position to forward. He did less ball-handling and more rebounding. Also, he took many of his shots with his back to the basket, instead of facing it. It took some getting used to, but eventually Vince got the hang of playing forward. He averaged 25 points and 11 rebounds a game. The Bucs went 30–2, and began to receive national recognition as one of the very best high-school teams in the country. Looking back, Vince really appreciates Coach Brinkerhoff's decision to move him to forward. "I now have post moves that give me an advantage over most shooting guards," he says.

Vince received a lot of credit for his team's success, and he deserved it. He was a true team player. Vince knew he could get a good shot every time down the court. But he wanted to get his teammates involved. Often he gave up sure baskets so that another player could get a chance. By the time the state playoffs rolled around, *everyone* was confident in their abilities. Vince and his teammates were a well-oiled machine.

Against the Jacksonville Mandarins in the playoffs, Coach Brinkerhoff decided to let the world see what he

Did You Know?

Charlie Brinkerhoff was also Vince's history teacher. He says Vince brought a lot to class discussions. "We were talking one day about the problems people have relating to other people," he recalls. "Vince said we needed to learn that it's important to accept people for what they are, but that it doesn't mean we have to become what they are."

and the other Bucs knew Vince could really do. Before the game, he instructed his star player to take every decent shot that came his way. Vince followed these instructions and poured in 35 points—in the first half! He finished with 47 points and 13 rebounds. When the final buzzer sounded, Vince was mobbed by his teammates. But he was embarrassed. "I felt like I was ball-hogging," he says. "Coach Brinkerhoff said to take every good, open shot I got, and the shot was falling in."

America's Most Wanted

"He has the heart of a champion."
— PREP BASKETBALL EXPERT BOB GIBBONS

Vince had a great senior year, both on and off the court. He enjoyed his courses (getting Bs or better), he was the most popular kid in school, the most heavily recruited basketball player in the state, and the drum major in the school's marching band. He not only called the shots for the band, he also wrote the songs they performed at halftime. "I know a lot of people laugh at the job," Vince says, "but it's more leadership than any of them realize."

One college, Bethune-Cookman, offered Vince a full musical scholarship. The recruiter said he could play basketball, too, if he felt like it. The other 80 schools that contacted Vince were less interested in his musical abilities. They wanted him to play basketball. Those schools included Duke, North Carolina, Florida, and Florida State. Vince decided to play his last season and then make up his mind.

And what a season it was! Vince continued to develop his gifts. He was the first player in the gym every day, and the last to leave. Coach Brinkerhoff jokes that he almost had to pry the ball out of Vince's hands. Early in the year, the Bucs rose into the nation's Top 20 list, and Mainland was invited to the country's most prestigious tournaments.

Vince learned early that altering a player's shot is just as good as blocking it.

At the Coca-Cola/KMOX Shootout in St. Louis, the Collinsville Kahoks—a top team from Missouri—unveiled a special zone defense designed specifically to shut Vince down. Frustrated, he committed three fouls and was forced to take a seat on the bench. Rather than pouting, Vince watched the game, analyzed his opponents, and devised a way to beat the zone. First, however, he needed to send a message to the Kahoks.

Vince went back into the game and rocked the arena with a reverse dunk. Next, he rejected three Collinsville shots in a row. With the defense in disarray, Vince "stretched" it by hitting a series of three-pointers, then spent the rest of the game cutting through the openings he created and dishing off to wide-open teammates. Mainland scored 21 of the game's final 25 points for an easy victory.

A few weeks later, during another important tournament, Vince chipped a bone in his right wrist when a defender fouled him on a dunk. No problem. He had the wrist heavily taped and padded to protect it against further damage, then continued to play lefthanded. He hit several shots, including four free throws. "I even got a southpaw dunk," Vince says proudly.

In most games, though, Vince was happy to let the other Bucs grab the spotlight. As the team continued to win, however, Vince's teammates became so confident that

COVER BOY

Vince was rated as the nation's sixth-best high-school senior by BLUE CHIP ILLUSTRATED, and was compared to Michael Jordan by Bob Gibbons, one of the sport's best talent scouts. Vince also appeared on the cover of STUDENT SPORTS magazine.

sometimes they did not bother to look for him when the team needed a big shot. Vince's stats were actually lower than they were in his junior year!

Coach Brinkerhoff started to worry. He called a special team meeting and asked Vince to stand up. "Let me introduce you to Vince Carter," he said. "He's an All-American. All of you are good basketball players, but Vince Carter is a great player. If you think you are better than he is, we'll run an isolation against you, and after you get the Nike print off your forehead, then we'll see how you rate."

The players got the message. For the rest of the year, whenever the Bucs had a key possession, they looked for Vince first. Mainland cruised to the state championship, with Vince scoring 22 points, hauling down 16 rebounds, and swatting 10 shots in the final. Vince was named Florida's "Mr. Basketball" as the state's top high-school player, and made the *USA Today*, *Parade Magazine*, and McDonald's All-America teams.

After the season, Vince turned his attention to college. Florida basketball fans expected him to attend Florida or Florida State. They were angry to learn that he was leaning toward North Carolina, which had a superior basketball program and Dean Smith, a legendary coach. When Vince made it official and chose UNC, he explained why. "If I just wanted to be the star of the team, I probably would go to Florida or Florida State," he told reporters. "But I'm preparing myself for beyond college. I dream about making the NBA."

One Leap Forward, Two Steps Back

chapter 4

"That guy jumps out of the gym!"
— SAM OAKEY, HIGH-SCHOOL ALL-AMERICAN

Before Vince Carter pulled on the Carolina blue and white uniform of the UNC Tar Heels, he had some more basketball to play. His first stop was the McDonald's All-America Game, which features the country's most exciting college-bound seniors. Prior to the game, Vince wrote another chapter in his legend during the Slam Dunk Contest. He received perfect scores on six dunks, and brought the fans to their feet on every attempt—including a successful one-handed, 360-degree jam

Vince poses for an official photo during his freshman year at UNC.

Vince was expected to fill the shoes of shot-blocker Rasheed Wallace, who left for the NBA in 1995.

and another that saw him leave the floor behind the foul line.

Vince was mobbed by the other players after every dunk. Even Kevin Garnett, who tried in vain to keep up with Vince, had to bow to the new king. "I just wanted to participate and have a little fun," says Vince humbly. "What really was a good time was having fun with the guys on the side."

Vince also got his first taste of international competition that year. He joined Team USA at the Junior World Championships in Athens, Greece. The strange food, the travel, and the time change threw all of the young Americans off their game, and the team finished seventh in the tournament.

When Vince returned to the United States, he had just a couple of weeks to prepare for his freshman year at North Carolina. He was amazed to find that the hype surrounding his arrival had already begun—and he was a little annoyed when he learned that TV channel ESPN had already predicted he would leave school early to join the NBA. One day he was watching MTV and saw a bunch of people wearing number 15 UNC jerseys. "What the heck is going on?" Vince wondered. "I haven't even started college yet!"

Once Vince arrived at the Chapel Hill campus, things only got worse. Students would follow him from class to class and yell things like, "You're our new God!" The problem, Vince soon realized, was that the previous spring the team had lost two of

"Vince had to get adjusted to the defense and all the hype. To digest that at an early age is very hard. He just did an outstanding job."
ADEMOLA OKULAJA

the most talented players it ever had—sophomores Jerry Stackhouse and Rasheed Wallace. The Tar Heels had just gone to the Final Four in the NCAA Tour-nament, and Coach Dean Smith had won at least 20 games a sea-son for 25 years. If UNC was going to keep its streak alive, its famous freshman would have to have a big year.

Coach Smith had recruited two other talented freshmen to help restock the Tar Heels lineup—forwards Antawn Jamison and Ademola Okulaja. They would join three returning starters—center Serge Zwikker, shooting guard Dante Calabria, and point guard Jeff McInnis. The experts were predicting an off-year for Carolina, but the players were confident. They believed they had the right mix to make it back to the NCAA Tournament.

Early in the season, the Tar Heels scored impressive wins over tough teams from Vanderbilt and Michigan State, and narrowly lost to Villanova. Then they reeled off 9 wins in their next 10 games, including an overtime victory over Maryland, one of UNC's main rivals in the Atlantic Coast Conference (ACC). Coach Smith worked his freshmen into the lineup carefully, making sure they were in situations where they were

"I want to be a guy who's dangerous inside and out-side...and also has a little flair on his dunks."

VINCE CARTER

likely to succeed. Vince played well in most games. Against North Carolina State, he only missed one shot and finished with 18 points.

Vince felt great about his fast start, and believed it was time to step up his game. That meant occasionally breaking away from Coach Smith's team philosophy. The Carolina system was designed to avoid mistakes, but in doing so it sometimes limited what the best players could do. In the 1980s, for instance, no one really knew how good Michael Jordan was because the team's system did not encourage him to "freelance" and go one-on-one.

As the Tar Heels began playing the toughest part of their schedule, and as the games got tighter, Vince tried to do too much by himself. Instead of working the ball around for a good shot, he often took it right to the basket. When his drives were stopped by Carolina's ACC rivals, he would get

Darvin Ham of Texas Tech shatters a backboard— and UNC's dream of an NCAA title—during UNC's first-round defeat in 1996.

dejected and forget to hustle back on defense. And instead of tightening up his man-to-man defense, opponents were finding it easier to fake him out and slip by.

Eventually, Coach Smith benched Vince and played the other freshmen more. Okulaja, who replaced Vince in the starting lineup, finished the season strong, and Jamison did so well he was voted ACC Freshman of the Year. Still, the Tar Heels lost 8 of their last 17 games—including an embarrassing defeat in the first round of the ACC Tournament—and then got blown out by Texas Tech early in the NCAA Tournament.

Vince looked back on his lost season and realized he still had a lot to learn about basketball and teamwork. He decided to stay in Chapel Hill over summer break and work on his game with some of the other Tar Heels. Before the break began, Vince received a call from a former Tar Heel who needed help running a local basketball camp. His name was Michael Jordan.

Did You Know?

After Vince was benched, rumors spread that he wanted to transfer to another school. Nonsense, says Vince. "I was frustrated, yes, but I never considered backing out."

Getting with the Program

"I was used to being
'The Man' on the team."

— VINCE CARTER

Working next to Michael Jordan every day was the best basketball education Vince Carter would ever get. Jordan was coming off his fourth NBA championship with the Chicago Bulls, but a few years earlier the superstar had become disenchanted with the NBA and actually left the game for almost two seasons. Now he was back in love with basketball, and it showed. Vince could see the joy, energy, commitment, and sacrifice that went into everything Jordan

Michael Jordan conducts a clinic at his basketball camp.

> *"I thought he was progressing at an excellent pace, and everybody else said, 'What's wrong with Vince Carter?' Well, that means their expectations were unrealistic and uninformed."*
> **DEAN SMITH**

did. It made Vince forget about the past and get excited about the future. He now understood what it took to be a star in the NBA, and he knew he had it in him.

Jordan unlocked something magical in Vince, and his teammates noticed it as soon as fall practice began. On offense, he finally felt like he was part of the flow. On defense, his footwork and anticipation were better than ever. After the team's first game, in which Vince scored 20 points and grabbed 8 rebounds, reporters wanted to know all about the "new" Vince Carter.

Coach Smith explained that Vince was right where he should be. Most highly recruited freshmen come to college with an unrealistic idea of how quickly they will adjust to big-time basketball. They need a "cool down" period the way Vince did. Now was just the right time for his sophomore sensation to start heating up.

Vince could sense his game coming together, and Coach Smith's vote of confidence did wonders for him. He played with passion and purpose, but stayed within the team's plan. Vince learned how to control his natural aggressiveness on the court. Instead of forcing plays that were not there, he saved his greatest plays for when rebounds were up for grabs or loose balls were rolling on the floor. Vince was at his best against the Tar Heels' toughest ACC opponents. In a game with Wake Forest, he exploded for 26 points. He poured in 20 during a key win over Clemson.

Vince's development came at the same time that freshman Ed Cota showed he was ready to handle the point-guard position. Coach Smith moved the smart, slick-passing

Vince cannot believe how close the Tar Heels came to winning it all in 1997.

Cota into a starting role, moved point guard Shammond Williams to shooting guard, and moved Vince into the small forward slot. Vince dusted off his old high-school moves and took to his new position quickly. UNC's "African connection"—Okulaja and Makhtar Ndiaye— played fabulously coming off the bench, enabling the Tar Heels to roll through the regular season with 21 wins.

In the ACC Tournament, Carolina handled Virginia, Wake Forest, and North Carolina State easily to claim the conference championship. In the NCAA Tournament, some were predicting the red-hot Heels would win it all. Carolina won its first-round game easily, against Fairfield. It was Coach Smith's 877th career victory, which tied him with Adolph Rupp for the most wins in Division I history. Smith got the record two days later, when his team beat Colorado by 17 points.

In the third round, Vince had a monster game against the University of California. Every time the Golden Bears looked for a path to the basket, it seemed as if Vince was already there. His defense totally disrupted California's offense, and his 14 points nailed down the win for Carolina. Vince repeated his fine performance in the Regional Final against Louisville. He scored 18 points, grabbed 7 rebounds, recorded 5 assists, and was all over the floor in a 20-point blowout. The Tar Heels had made it to the Final Four!

Unfortunately for North Carolina, their amazing run ended in the national semi-final game. A young and talented Arizona team—led by Miles Simon and Mike Bibby—outplayed the Tar Heels and squeezed out a 66–58 victory. Vince had a great game, scoring more than a third of the team's points, but it just was not good enough. Arizona went on to win the national championship.

Vince decided to hang around school during the summer of 1997. Once again, he and his teammates decided to stay in Chapel Hill and continue polishing their games. One afternoon, while he and the other Tar Heels were playing a pickup game, a gangly young man walked into the gym hoping to join them. He and Vince instantly struck up a friendship. His name was Tracy McGrady, and he had just finished his junior

year at Auburndale High School in Florida. Vince recognized the name immediately. McGrady was one of the top prep players in the country, and there were whispers that he might skip college and go directly to the pros if he continued to progress during his senior year at Auburndale.

A week later, McGrady was attending a family reunion. An older woman, hearing that he was a basketball player, asked if he knew her grandson, who played basketball, too. "Who's that?" McGrady asked.

"Vince Carter," the woman replied. Tracy and Vince were cousins!

Vince and his cousin, Tracy McGrady.

New Man at the Top

chapter 6

"Dad's gone. Now uncle is going to step in. Who better to take over?"

— VINCE CARTER

The Tar Heels began practicing for the 1997–1998 season with one goal: winning the national championship. All the key players from the previous year's Final Four squad were back, except center Serge Zwikker. He was replaced by Brendan Haywood, 7 feet (213 centimeters) tall with a feathery touch around the basket. Just when everything seemed to be falling into place, however, the team was hit with the shocking news that Dean Smith was retiring. Coach Smith had been on the Carolina sidelines for 36 years, and he just could not do it anymore. Replacing him would be his faithful assistant, Bill Guthridge.

Although shaken by the change, Vince and the other players were happy that the job was staying

Bill Guthridge works the sideline.

"in the family." Guthridge was like a favorite uncle to the players, and he promised not to change a thing. Vince liked the new coach's inner fire. "He may look like a mild-mannered guy," says Vince, "but he's more like a warrior at times. If he's talking to you about diving for a loose ball, he might dive after one, too."

The team stayed focused on its goals and began the season with an amazing 17-victory streak. Vince and Antawn Jamison made up the most lethal forward combination in college basketball. Both stars shot better than 60 percent from the floor, killing opponents with drives and dunks as well as three-pointers. Vince was the team's most versatile defender. Some nights he would take the other team's point guard. Other nights he would guard a high-scoring power forward.

After losing an overtime game to Maryland, Carolina reeled off nine more wins to stand at 26–1. In the ACC Tournament, the Tar Heels rolled to their second-straight conference title. Vince scored 16 points in the clinching game, an 83–68 win over the Duke Blue Devils. When the NCAA Tournament schedule was announced, Carolina was one of the number-one seeds. A return to the Final Four seemed assured. From there, they would get their shot at the national championship.

Vince goes up for 2 of his 20 points against Michigan State in the 1998 NCAA Tournament.

The Tar Heels sank Navy in the first round, but struggled to beat UNC-Charlotte in a nerve-wracking overtime game. Vince came through again and again in this contest, finishing with 24 points. In the next round, Vince's 20 points and 10 rebounds helped Carolina win a tough battle against Michigan State. In the fourth round, UNC defeated the talented Huskies from the University of Connecticut. In this game, Vince scored only 12 points, but allowed UConn star Richard Hamilton to score on less than one out of every four shots.

Carolina had made the Final Four, and now was just two wins away from its goal. Vince was totally pumped to play, but his teammates failed to follow his lead. They performed poorly in the first half of their game against the underdog Utah Utes, and at halftime UNC found itself behind by 13 points. Vince tried to get his team back in the game in the second half, and ended up with a team-high 21 points. But Utah held on to advance to the championship game.

Vince was disappointed during the weeks following UNC's Final Four loss, but still determined. There was no way the Tar Heels would fall again if they reached the Final Four. Vince started to have his doubts, however, when Antawn Jamison decided to give up his final year at school and enter the NBA Draft. His friend's decision caused him to rethink his own future. Without Antawn, opponents would hound Vince all game long. It was one thing to draw double-teams in high school. It would be a lot worse in the ACC.

Did You Know?

Vince signed a contract with his mother when he left for college in 1995. It stated that no matter what happened, he would earn a diploma. Although she supported her son's decision to turn pro, Michelle reminded him of their deal. Vince held up his end of the bargain, returning to complete the courses he needed for his degree.

When Vince closed his eyes and pictured his senior season, he did not see success and happiness anymore. Maybe, he thought, this is the time to go.

Leaving school was an easy choice for Jamison, but for Vince it was more complicated. He loved campus life. He was doing great in his classes and was just a couple of credits short of earning his degree in African-American studies. As in high school, Vince was one of the most popular people in school. And his high-school friend, Cori Brown, was both his roommate and manager of the basketball team. That was a lot to give up.

Vince talked it over with his parents, and with Bill Guthridge and Dean Smith. Each told him to follow his dream. Still, he could hardly believe his own words when he made the announcement to leave the University of North Carolina. Vince was headed for the NBA.

Vince eyes the basket as he launches himself for a big dunk.

First Impressions

chapter 7

"He can do things in the air most people can't do on the ground."

— TORONTO GENERAL MANAGER
GREG GRUNWALD

D raft day in the NBA is one of the most interesting in all of sports. The experts spend all spring predicting which teams will take which players, then hold their breath with the rest of the fans while they wait to hear the final results. There are always surprises, and there is a lot of wheeling and dealing behind the scenes. Some teams know exactly the player they want, but do not own a pick high enough to get him. Others have high picks, but cannot decide which player to take. Very often, teams in these situations contact each other. At the 1998 NBA Draft, the Golden State Warriors and Toronto Raptors were talking about Vince Carter.

The Warriors picked fourth and the Raptors fifth. As luck would have it, Golden State's choice came down to two players: Antawn Jamison and Vince. The Raptors wanted Vince. They needed an exciting star to awaken interest in the team, and Vince had much more to offer in this area than Jamison.

When the Warriors decided to take Vince, the Raptors quickly grabbed Jamison. Toronto's general manager, Greg Grunwald, immediately offered Jamison and $500,000 for Vince. He knew Golden State could use the cash. The Warriors, who later

Vince joined Tracy McGrady on the Raptors after turning pro in 1998. Tracy had gone right from high school to the NBA.

claimed they had wanted Jamison all along, accepted the offer and just like that, Vince was a Raptor. Vince could not have been happier. Although Toronto can get a bit cold in the winter, it is a very cool town with a lot to do. Also, the Raptors had Tracy McGrady on the roster. Vince's cousin had indeed skipped college and had been drafted by Toronto the year before. "It's gonna be the Tracy and Vince show," he and his cousin told the press.

Although the Raptors were just three years old, they were putting together a team that was designed to compete with the NBA's best. Vince would join a lineup that included two veteran rebounders, Charles Oakley and Kevin Willis. The team's point-guard job was up in the air, but the shooting-guard job would be manned by Doug Christie and Dee Brown. Vince was ticketed for the small forward slot.

Normally, NBA teams have a chance to come together during summer training camp. The players get to work on their timing, the coaches get to introduce new plays, and newcomers have a chance to get used to their new surroundings. Unfortunately, the summer of 1998 was not normal. The NBA's owners wanted to make big changes in their working agreement with the players, and the players wanted things to stay the same. When the two sides failed to budge, the owners "locked out" the players, meaning that they refused to open training camps. As the dispute dragged on into the fall

Vince and Coach Butch Carter talk strategy during a game.

and winter, the entire season was in jeopardy of being canceled.

Vince tried his best to keep his game sharp, and managed to practice with some of his future teammates. But without coaches, these were no more than pickup games. When the two sides finally settled in early 1999, the season was cut from 82 to 50 games, and teams were given almost no time to prepare. Vince hurried to Toronto, where Coach Butch Carter faced the difficult task of blending a lot of new players into a new playing system.

The lack of practice showed when the season started. The veterans and young players did not always blend smoothly, and Coach Carter never knew what he could expect from his bench players from one night to the next. The one thing that held everything together was the play of the team's rookie sensation, Vince Carter. From opening night, when he scored 16 points in a win over the Boston Celtics, the team looked to Vince whenever it needed a lift.

In March, the Raptors started coming together. The team completed the first winning month in its history, with Vince playing a role in every victory. In a thrilling win over the Detroit Pistons, he took over the fourth quarter and poured in 17 points. A few days later, Vince was named NBA Player of the Week—a rare honor for a rookie. As the season wore on, the Raptors hovered at the .500 level, and were just behind the sputtering New York Knicks for the final playoff berth in the league's Eastern Conference.

Vince was spectacular down the stretch. Whereas many first-year players "disappear" in the final few minutes of close games, he took charge. He hit an amazing 20-foot (6-meter) turnaround jumper to sink the Indiana Pacers at the buzzer, then forced

Vince throws one down against the Celtics. Plays like this made the TV highlights night after night.

Washington sharp-shooter Mitch Richmond to throw up an air ball with time expiring in Toronto's very next game.

These were not the plays fans saw on television, however. Vince was becoming a national sensation because of his high-flying dunks. Every time the Raptors played—whether they won or lost—the highlights always seemed to feature Vince soaring through the air and jamming the ball into the basket. It got so that fans just thought of him as a dunking machine. They did not see the other parts of his game— the skills he had worked so hard to develop.

Other NBA players knew how good Vince was. And how good he was going to be. They talked about how he had improved his outside shooting, and how comfortable he was driving to his left. They liked his instincts around the backboard, too, not just above the rim.

The Knicks heated up and the Raptors faded down the stretch, and that last play-off spot disappeared. After their final game, Vince pledged that Toronto fans would be watching a playoff team a year later. Despite all the obstacles, they had come close in 1999. In 2000, he said, the Raptors would be a legitimate contender.

Did You Know?

Vince was honored as the NBA's 1999 Rookie of the Year. Besides bringing down 5.7 rebounds and handing out 3.0 assists per game, his scoring average of 18.3 points led all first-year players. He donated the money he won to Mainland High School.

Promise Keeper

chapter 8

*"We are going to make it happen.
We want to make Toronto a basketball city."*

— VINCE CARTER

A lot of players hate listening to criticism. Vince Carter is not one of those players. In addition to the high praise he received after his great rookie year, he also heard a few negative comments about his game. Vince's outside shot, the experts felt, was not yet up to NBA standards. And although he could make the great plays, he did not always make the routine ones. Vince knew there was only one way to fix these problems, and that was to practice.

To improve his aim and endurance, and to build the muscles he would need to get through a long, tiring NBA season, Vince went to the gym every day during the summer of 1999 and shot at least 1,000 jump shots. "Shoot, shoot, shoot," he smiles. "Until I couldn't shoot anymore."

When Vince arrived at training camp he was 10 pounds (4.5 kilograms) heavier. Thanks to his shooting routine, every ounce of that was strong, supple muscle added to his arms and back. The Raptors were stronger, too. Added to the front line was Antonio Davis, a monster rebounder and

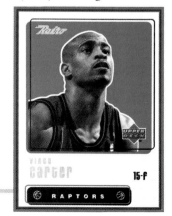

Collectors have gone crazy for Vince's cards—even ones that do not show him dunking.

Vince put on a show against the Knicks early in the 1999–2000 season, scoring 36 points. They would meet again in the playoffs.

defensive player who could substitute for the aging Kevin Willis and Charles Oakley. And Tracy McGrady was ready to step up and play a more important role. He too had added bulk to his long frame, and his quickness off the floor gave the Raptors a dynamic scoring and rebounding threat they had not had the year before.

Vince and Tracy would have extra room to operate thanks to another new-comer, Dell Curry. The veteran was one of the league's top three-point shooters. When Curry was in the game, opponents would have to spread out more to defend him. The team's lone weakness was still at point guard, where Alvin Williams split time with Muggsy Bogues. Both were capable of great play, but neither was good enough to claim the full-time job.

Once again, Vince predicted the Raptors would contend—not just for a playoff spot, but for the Eastern Conference crown. The Knicks, Miami Heat, and Indiana Pacers were getting old. First place, insisted Vince, was not as crazy as people thought. In time, he had his teammates believing. Whether he knew it or not, Vince was becoming a team leader.

Vince also was becoming a little annoyed with his reputation as the league's "human highlight film." It suggested that he was a one-dimensional player; he wanted to be known as a complete one. "Dunkers come and go," he explains. "You can go down to the playground and find a bunch of guys who do fancy dunks. The great players excel at all aspects of the game. That's what I want to be."

Vince's through-the-legs dunk at the 2000 All-Star Game is still hard to believe.

Carter was all that and more as the Raptors got off to a roaring start. The team won 7 of its first 10 games. Vince contributed on both ends of the floor, scoring 20 or more points eight times. He played with energy and enthusiasm that inspired his teammates and really brought the fans into the game. The high point of the season's first month was Toronto's mind-boggling win over the Los Angeles Lakers, who had the best team in the NBA. Vince scored 34 during this memorable matchup with Shaquille O'Neal and Kobe Bryant. At the end of the month, the Raptors were right where Vince predicted they would be, in first place!

During Vince's first NBA season, opponents were often willing to let him operate freely. They figured that, being a rookie, he would make rookie mistakes. Also, when Vince suddenly took charge it sometimes threw off the timing of the other Raptors. Now the Raptors *looked* to Vince to take charge. Instead of messing up their timing, he created opportunities. This forced other teams to plan strategies for stopping Vince. Once and a while they did. But more often than not Vince came out on top.

In the season's second month, Vince scored a total of 71 points in back-to-back games against the San Antonio Spurs and Cleveland Cavaliers. Later he shook the team out of a slump with a 35-point outburst against the Houston Rockets. In January he lit up the Milwaukee Bucks for 47 points. In this game, Vince burned Ray Allen again and again. Allen had just been selected for the final spot on the team that would compete in the 2000 Olympics. Vince and his teammates felt he deserved the spot more than Allen, and this performance certainly backed them up.

As January ended, Vince received some startling news. The fan-voting for the NBA All-Star Game had been tabulated, and he was the leading vote-getter, with 1.9 million. The only player ever to receive more votes was Michael Jordan—the man to whom Vince was being compared more and more.

Those comparisons only increased during the Saturday Slam Dunk com-

The Carter File

VINCE'S FAVORITE...

Food	Steak and Pasta
Book	*The Autobiography of Malcolm X*
TV Show	ESPN's SportsCenter
Player	Julius Erving. "I'm still a big fan of Dr. J."

During the Olympics, Vince got the urge to try a new sport. "I had this inspiration, this burning desire to high jump—no training or anything. I just wanted to try it."

petition at All-Star Weekend. Vince, who for a few moments had actually *been* a Golden State Warrior, treated Warrior fans in Oakland to a little of what they were missing. He left his mark on the contest with two unforgettable dunks. For the first, Tracy McGrady served as Vince's "spotter." Tracy threw a bounce pass to his cousin, who caught it in midair, passed the ball through his legs, and then slammed it one-handed. Vince's second masterpiece was a display of sheer power. Starting near mid-court, he ran to the foul line, took off, and dunked the ball hard as the crowd went crazy. Needless to say, he won the competition.

Vince was the hottest athlete in team sports. He already had endorsement deals with Gatorade, Sky Box, Kellogg's, and Spalding. Now more lucrative offers came rolling in, and demand for public appearances and interviews skyrocketed. Superstar Grant Hill, who had the misfortune of being called "the next Jordan" a few years earlier, watched what was happening to Vince and could only shake his head. "I feel sorry for him," said Hill. "He's going to be exhausted."

> "Once he starts knocking down the jumper consistently and plays better defense on the perimeter, look out!"
>
> **CHARLES OAKLEY**

Vince did not feel tired. But the edge was starting to come off his game. Right after the All-Star break the Raptors played the Indiana Pacers. Jalen Rose outscored Vince, 23–4, in the first half! Coach Butch Carter accused Vince of trying to rest on the court, and threatened to cut his minutes if he could not go all-out all the time. Vince sucked it up and got his head back into basketball. In a game against the Phoenix Suns he scored 51 points, with the final basket sealing a 103–102 win with time running out.

The Phoenix game ignited the Raptors, who went on to win 10 of their next 11. During this stretch, Vince did it all. He shot well from outside, drove strong to the hoop, scored off his post-up moves, and found the open man whenever opponents double-teamed him. Something even more exciting happened over the course of Toronto's hot streak. More and more, the league's referees began whistling defenders for fouling Vince. Usually, a player has to be in the league for several years before he is "protected" by the refs. But Vince's superstar aura had convinced officials to give him special treatment usually reserved for the NBA's elite performers.

You might think that this would be fun for Vince. But just the opposite was true. Knowing they would be whistled for even the slightest foul, defenders decided to "make their fouls count" by roughing up Vince and attempting to injure or intimidate him. In a return match with the Houston Rockets, Vince was pushed to the floor several times. He refused to back down, however, and responded by beating the Rockets on a slam dunk with 1.6 seconds left.

By the end of the regular season, Vince heard himself being compared to Michael Jordan almost every day. He tried everything he knew to make people stop, partly because he was tired of hearing it, but mostly because he felt his teammates were not getting the attention *they* deserved. "I am who I am," he says. "There is a lot of pressure in being the 'Next Man.' I'm my own person and I want to establish my own identity.... I'm honored by the comparison, but I want to be me."

Playoff Blues

chapter **9**

> *"He'll be one of the greats in this league for a long time."*
>
> — KNICKS COACH JEFF VAN GUNDY

oronto finished the 1999–2000 season in third place in the Central Division and drew the New York Knicks as a first-round playoff opponent. The Raptors knew they were in for a war. New York was a team of well-coached, gritty veterans. The Knicks knew how to make other teams play their slow, grinding style; a young, inexperienced club like the Raptors would have to avoid being lured into this trap.

Knicks coach Jeff Van Gundy decided to force his counterpart, Butch Carter, into making big changes in the game plan that had worked so well for the Raptors during the regular season. Van Gundy had heard that several Toronto veterans had questioned Carter's ability to coach in the postseason, and gambled that the Raptors would not respond to his changes.

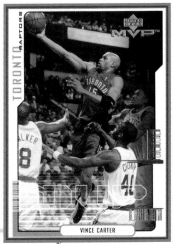

As this Upper Deck card shows, Vince was the Raptors' MVP for 1999–2000.

This was typical of the rough playoff series between the Raptors and Knicks. Vince and Charlie Ward battle for the ball, while Muggsy Bogues gets flattened.

Prior to the first game, Coach Carter got into a war of words with Knicks big man Marcus Camby. Camby had once played for Carter in Toronto, and the two had never seen eye-to-eye. Carter went so far as to file a lawsuit against Camby, which caused a great swirl of publicity. The craziness that followed seemed to distract the Raptors, who promptly lost the opener. It did not help that Vince had one of his worst days as a pro. The Knicks jabbed and jostled him, threw him off his game, and then dared him to beat them. Vince fell for this trick, playing angry and making just 3 of 20 shots.

In the second game of this best-of-five series, Vince bounced back and played very well. No matter what the Knicks tried, he had the right answer. It looked as if the Raptors would knot the series at 1–1, but New York came back and took a one-point lead with seconds to play. With one last chance to win, Toronto inbounded the ball to Vince, who instantly drew two defenders. Out of the corner of his eye, he noticed Dee Brown wide open in the corner. He whipped the ball over to Brown, who lofted a jump shot as time ran out. The ball clanked off the rim, and Toronto was down 2–0.

After the game, Vince was criticized for not taking charge and not driving to the hoop. Fans felt that he had a better chance of drawing a foul than

Did You Know?

Vince was shocked when his trusted agent, Tank Black, was indicted on a number of criminal charges in February 2000. Vince turned his business dealings over to the person he trusted most, his mom. After the season, he signed with International Management Group (IMG).

Brown had of hitting such a long shot. Of course, had Brown hit the shot, Vince would have been applauded for his unselfish play. But that is the way it goes at playoff time—

This probably won't be the last magazine cover Vince, Kobe Bryant, and Allen Iverson share.

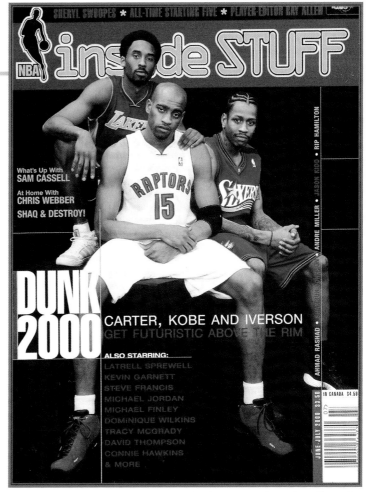

you're either an idiot or a genius. "I wanted to take it, but they denied it," he says of the play. "So I had to go to 'Plan B' and find the open man."

Game Three saw the Knicks beat a demoralized Raptors team. New York concentrated on stopping Vince again, and held him to just 15 points. Taking advantage of this situation was Tracy McGrady who stepped up and had a big game. Alas, in the end it was not enough, as Toronto lost, 87–80, and was eliminated from the postseason.

A first-round playoff loss was not the end that Vince had in mind to his "breakthrough" season. But it was a breakthrough season nonetheless. As promised, Vince had led Toronto to the playoffs. He had increased his scoring to 25.7 points per game, and had earned the respect of everyone in the league.

Vince still had his critics. Michael Jordan, for one, thought he needed to pay more attention to his defense. Yet Jordan had little doubt that Vince was only a season or two away from being a complete, championship-caliber player. He had the drive and the talent, and he wanted every win to be a *team* win. Vince, observed Jordan, just needed to learn when to share the load and when to take command—the same process he went through as a young NBA star.

Golden Guy

chapter 10

"It's not easy when everyone wants a piece of you."

— GRANT HILL

The summer of 2000 is one Vince Carter will never forget. When the Raptors were bounced from the playoffs, Vince figured the offseason would be a quiet one. Was he ever wrong! The first bit of bad news came from a judge, who ordered him to repay more than $13 million in endorsement money he had received from Puma to wear its basketball shoes. Early in his career, Vince had tried to wear the sneakers, but found they hurt his feet. No matter what Puma engineers tried, they could not make a pair that Vince liked. So he simply stopped wearing Pumas. The company demanded its money back, and through the courts they got it. As usual, Vince took the decision in stride.

Did You Know?

During the summer of 2000, Vince made one of the greatest moves ever, but only the Dream Teamers were around to see it. "The first day of camp," remembers team official Stu Jackson, "there's a lob pass going out of bounds. He reaches for it with his right hand, somehow twists around, and jams it down hard. Stopped the practice cold!"

"I'm still going to be me," he says. "Take the blow, turn the other cheek, move on."

Veteran Steve Smith, who shared some valuable secrets with Vince in Sydney.

After writing that large, painful check, Vince got another slap in the face. This one came from a most unexpected place—his cousin, Tracy. The Raptors, fearing they would not be able to re-sign him the following year, had traded McGrady to the Orlando Magic. In a magazine interview, McGrady blasted the Raptors and said that he looked forward to "kicking Vince's butt." Vince was shocked. "I was surprised," he admits. "It hurt a little bit. But that's the way it goes. I've slept on it and it's over with."

The summer was not all bad. Vince got to spend some time in Chapel Hill, where he took courses toward earning his diploma. And he made the Olympic squad after all. Forward Tom Gugliotta had to withdraw for medical reasons, and Vince was selected to replace him. Vince joined the Dream Team in preparation for the Olympic Games in Sydney, Australia. The team included some of the best talent in the NBA, including Tim Duncan and Kevin Garnett.

A highlight of this period was the friendship Vince formed with guard Steve Smith. Smith, who is eight years older than Vince, had long been one of Vince's favorite players. They hit it off immediately. Vince knows he may be asked to play guard again, so he quizzed the veteran on some of the "little things" that made him successful in the NBA. Smith told Vince that stardom comes down to the stuff that is *not* glamorous— dedication and hard work, both on and off the court.

Before the Olympics started, Team USA traveled across the Pacific Ocean to play several warm-up games. The idea was to get used to the slightly different rules of international basketball, and also to become accustomed to the dramatic time

Vince became the top scorer on Team USA. This dunk over Frederic Weis is legendary.

change. Australia is 16 hours ahead of the United States. For instance, when it is noon in New York, it is four o'clock the next morning in Sydney.

In these games, Vince and his teammates discovered that times had changed in other ways. In 1992 the first Dream Team—starring Magic Johnson, Larry Bird, and Michael Jordan—had been the hit of the Olympics. At the 1996 games in Atlanta, the Dream Team caused less of a commotion, but had the crowd on its side because it was the home team. At the 2000 Olympics, the Dream Team was still the team to beat, but for the first time there were other countries that thought they had a chance of actually beating them. The U.S. players were challenged every time down the court, and they did not like it. In a game against Australia, Vince got into a shoving match with Andrew Gaze, Australia's most beloved player. As a result, Vince was booed by Aussie fans during his entire stay in their country. He had never been booed in his life.

Once the Olympics started, it was business as usual for the Americans. Although the games were close, Team USA swept through the competition to win the gold medal. During the tournament, Vince emerged as something of a team leader. He was the one reporters most often approached with questions, and on the court he led the national squad in scoring with 14.8 points per game. "I just gave it my all," he says. "I wasn't doing anything out of the ordinary."

Spectators at the USA-France game might disagree. In that contest, Vince pulled off what Olympic historians will probably be calling "The Dunk" for many, many years. Frederic Weis, France's 7-foot 2-inch (218-cm) center, moved into the lane to thwart one of Vince's drives to the basket. Instead of changing his path to the rim, Vince decided to go right through Weis. He lifted off and rose above the awestruck Frenchman, who could only watch as Vince sailed up and over him and crashed the ball through the hoop. The crowd went insane. So did Vince's teammates.

Although everyone expected Team USA to dominate, winning the gold medal still meant a lot to Vince. He had never won anything really important, and he still had a bad taste in his mouth from the playoffs. "It will heal a lot of bruises and bad spots in my mind," he said.

Vince and Kevin Garnett enjoy their gold medals.

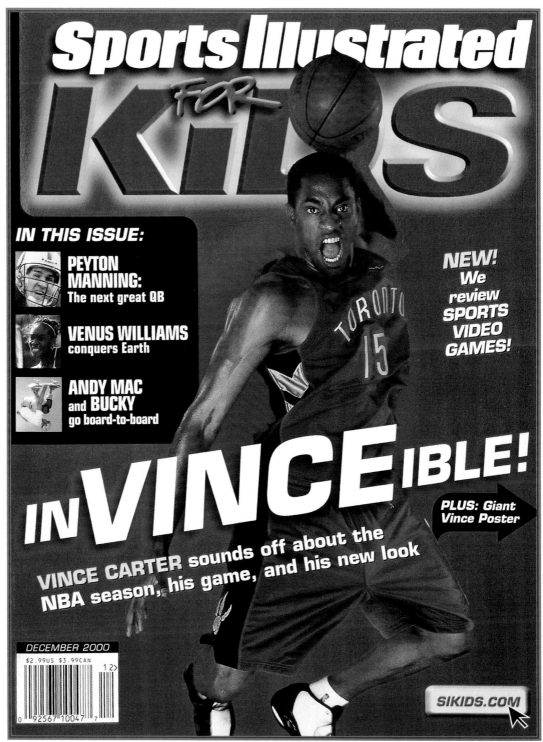

Millions of young fans got their first look at Vince's new hairstyle on the cover of **SPORTS ILLUSTRATED FOR KIDS.**

chapter 11

Solid Citizen

"He's not wearing braids, he doesn't have any tattoos. He's just a regular guy who comes out and works hard every night."

— TIM HARDAWAY

N o sooner had Vince returned from Sydney than it was time to get ready for his third NBA season. The Raptors had made an important move while he was away. Not surprisingly, Butch Carter was let go by the Raptors. He was replaced with Lenny Wilkens, a Hall of Fame player who also owns the league record for victories by a coach. That suited Vince just fine. "Lenny Wilkens is a mastermind of the game of basketball," he says. "It's going to be fun because he's accomplished so much."

During a season that saw a lot of players come and go, Wilkens carefully molded his team around Vince and stressed the fundamentals. Despite a constantly changing cast, the Raptors were among the NBA's best teams in

Lenny Wilkens watches the Raptors from the sideline.

Vince has set his sights on nothing less than an NBA championship. He knows he has work to do before he gets one.

assists, rebounds, and limiting turnovers. Toronto's weak point was still its defense, however. The team still lost a lot of games it should have won.

With Vince improving and the rest of the Raptors learning to play as a team under Wilkens, it should not be long before the Toronto Raptors are a year-in, year-out contender. Unlike some of the league's young stars, Vince has made the connection between hard work and success. This also enabled him to play through a series of minor injuries in 2000–2001. As Vince grows into his role of team leader, this will rub off on his teammates. And as Michael Jordan proved, if the star puts in the extra effort, everyone else will, too.

What can fans expect from Vince in the future? How good might he be one day? His outside shot should continue to improve, and he will become a smarter rebounder. On defense, he will learn how to read his opponents and keep a book on their best moves. And at both ends of the court, he will find ways to make the players around him

college *stats*

SEASON	SCHOOL	G	FG%	APG	RPG	PPG
1995–96	North Carolina	31	49.2	1.3	3.8	7.5
1996–97	North Carolina	34	52.5	2.4	4.5	13.0
1997–98	North Carolina	38	59.1	1.9	5.1	15.6
Total		**103**	**54.7**	**1.9**	**4.5**	**12.3**

pro *stats*

SEASON	TEAM	G	FG%	APG	RPG	PPG
1998–99	Raptors	50	45.0	3.0	5.7	18.3
1999–00	Raptors	82	46.5	3.9	5.8	25.7
Total		**132**	**46.0**	**3.6**	**5.8**	**22.9**

pro *highlights*

NBA Rookie of the Year	1999
Top All-Star Vote-Getter	2000
NBA Slam Dunk Champion	2000
Olympic Gold Medalist	2000
NBA All-Star	2000, 2001

a little better. In the end, that is what a superstar is—not someone who scores 30 points and makes all the highlight shows, but someone who finds a way for his team to win.

As for being the center of attention wherever he goes—both on and off the court—Vince says that is okay with him. If it takes the pressure off the rest of the team, he is willing to put up with it. Besides, he smiles, "I don't mind taking that challenge. I know every night they're coming for me, and that means I have to be on top of my game, whether it's scoring, passing, defending, or something else."

"I like to smile, even in intense situations. My opponents don't know how to react when they see me smile."

VINCE CARTER

basketball's new wave

Index